SPECIAL ★OPS II★
Navy SEAL Team Six
in Action

by Stephen Person

Consultant: Fred Pushies
U.S. Special Operations Forces Adviser

BEARPORT
PUBLISHING

New York, New York

Credits

Cover and Title Page, © United States Naval Special Warfare Command; 4, © Aero Graphics, Inc./Corbis; 5T, © Reuters/Stringer/Files; 5B, © Steve McCurry/Magnum Photos; 6T, © Yslb Pak/ZUMAPress/Newscom; 6B, © U.S. Navy Photo/Alamy; 7, © Pete Souza, Official White House Photographer; 8, © Louie Psihoyos/Corbis; 9, © U.S. DoD photo by Sgt. Aaron Rognstad; 10, © Time & Life Pictures/Getty Images; 11, © Naval History & Heritage Command, Washington D.C.; 12, © AP Photo/U.S. Navy; 13L, © AP Photo/Courtesy U.S. Sen. Bob Kerrey; 13R, © Najlah Feanny/Corbis; 14, © Bettmann/Corbis; 15, Courtesy of U.S. Government; 16, © Gary Kieffer/ZUMAPress/Newscom; 17, © Aaron Ansarov/Aurora Photos; 18, © Leif Skoogfors/Corbis; 19, © U.S. Navy photo by Photographer's Mate 1st Class Arlo K. Abrahamson; 20T, © U.S. Navy photo by Mass Communication Specialist 2nd Class Joshua T. Rodriguez/Released; 20B, © Jason Meyer/Alamy; 21, © MCCS Jeremy L. Wood; 22–23, © Reuters/Joseph Okanga; 24, © Sindelar/U.S. NAVY/SIPA/SIPA/Newscom; 25, © U.S. Navy photo; 26L, © Chuck Mussi/Corbis; 26R, © U.S. Navy photo by Mass Communication Specialist Seaman Apprentice Anthony Harding/Released; 27, © DoD photo by Senior Chief Petty Officer Andrew McKaskle, U.S. Navy; 28T, © Jim Sugar/Corbis; 28B, © U.S. Navy Photo/Alamy; 29TL, © Charles Neff, USN; 29TR, © Reuters/Andrew Burton; 29B, © Reuters/HO/USMC/Cpl. Eric R. Martin RCS/JJ.

Publisher: Kenn Goin
Editorial Director: Adam Siegel
Creative Director: Spencer Brinker
Design: Debrah Kaiser
Photo Researcher: We Research Pictures, LLC

Library of Congress Cataloging-in-Publication Data

Person, Stephen.
  Navy SEAL Team Six in action / by Stephen Person ; consultant, Fred Pushies, U.S. Special Operations Forces Adviser.
      pages cm. — (Special ops II)
  Includes bibliographical references and index.
  Audience: Ages 7–12.
  ISBN-13: 978-1-61772-890-7 (library binding) — ISBN-10: 1-61772-890-X (library binding)
  1. United States. Navy. SEALs—Juvenile literature. I. Pushies, Fred J., 1952– II. Title.
  VG87.P48 2014
  359.9'84—dc23
                          2013011526

For more information, write to Bearport Publishing Company, Inc., 45 West 21st Street, Suite 3B, New York, New York 10010. Printed in the United States of America.

10 9 8 7 6 5 4 3 2 1

Contents

Midnight Raid

On the dark, moonless night of May 1, 2011, two Black Hawk helicopters crossed the border from Afghanistan into Pakistan. Crowded into both of the helicopters were members of the U.S. Navy SEAL Team Six. These were some of the most highly trained **special operations forces** in the world.

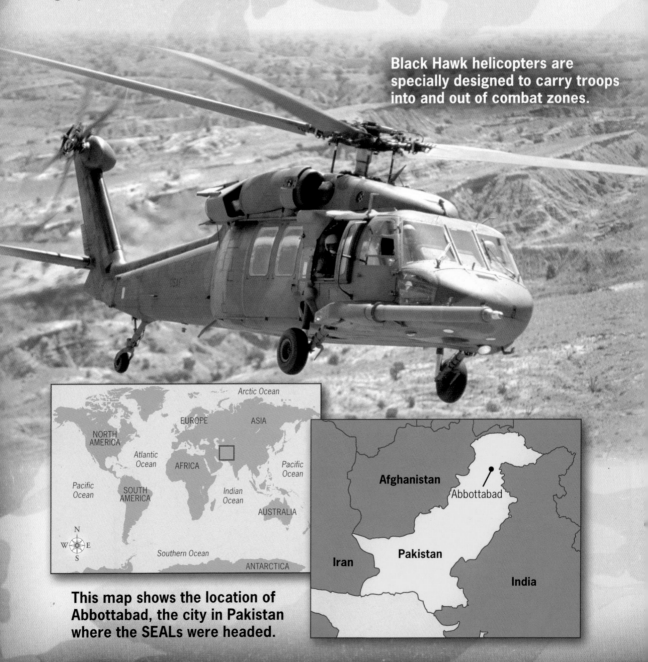

Black Hawk helicopters are specially designed to carry troops into and out of combat zones.

This map shows the location of Abbottabad, the city in Pakistan where the SEALs were headed.

When they reached the town of Abbottabad (uh-BOT-uh-*bod*), the Black Hawks swooped low over a group of buildings surrounded by high walls. This was the secret hideout of **terrorist** leader Osama bin Laden. The mission of SEAL Team Six was to go inside and get him. It wouldn't be easy, though. Bin Laden had successfully escaped capture for more than ten years.

Osama bin Laden was responsible for planning the September 11, 2001, terrorist attacks against the United States. The attacks killed more than 3,000 people.

In addition to flying planes into the World Trade Center in New York City on September 11, 2001 (shown below), terrorists also flew a plane into the Pentagon in Arlington, Virginia. Another plane crashed into a field in Pennsylvania after passengers fought off the terrorists.

Mission Accomplished

As the Black Hawks landed, the Team Six fighters jumped out. Soon, loud blasts filled the air. Someone from inside bin Laden's house had started shooting at the SEALs. Within moments, the SEALs charged inside the **compound** and up the stairs. When they reached the top floor, they found bin Laden. Immediately, one SEAL aimed his weapon at the terrorist. He fired one shot into bin Laden's chest and another above his left eye, killing him.

Osama bin Laden was hiding inside this compound in Pakistan.

Navy SEALs, such as the ones who were sent to capture bin Laden, are trained to fight in all kinds of settings.

The SEALs then quickly searched the building. They gathered papers and computer files that held valuable **intelligence** about the plans of bin Laden's terrorist group, **Al Qaeda**. About 40 minutes from the moment they landed, the SEALs jumped back into their helicopters and took off. They had accomplished their dangerous mission without losing a single man.

On the night of the bin Laden operation, President Barack Obama and his top advisers gathered in the White House to get updates on the action.

The Black Hawk helicopters used in the bin Laden operation were flown by another special operations group, the Army Night Stalkers.

Navy SEALs

Why did U.S. **military leaders** pick Navy SEALs to carry out the bin Laden mission? The job called for highly trained troops who could conduct top-secret missions behind **enemy lines**. It called for soldiers who could work as a team and react quickly to changing situations. In short, the job called for the Navy SEALs.

SEALs must be as comfortable in water as they are on land.

Navy SEALs are special operations forces that are trained to carry out missions on any type of **terrain**. In fact, the name *SEAL* is short for "Sea, Air, and Land Forces." Working in small groups, SEALs fight in cities and at sea. They **parachute** from planes, **scuba dive** in the ocean, and climb mountains—whatever it takes to complete their mission.

There are a total of about 2,500 active duty SEALs. They conduct operations all over the world.

Sliding down ropes from helicopters allows SEALs to land in hard-to-reach places.

Leading the Way

The history of the SEALs goes back to World War II (1939–1945), when the United States was fighting against Germany, Japan, and Italy. During that war, military leaders needed a team of special operations forces who would be able to help troops land on beaches controlled by the enemy. As a result, the Army and Navy formed the Scouts and Raiders.

Members of the Raiders training for landing invasions in 1942

The Scouts and Raiders took on incredibly dangerous missions, such as swimming up to enemy beaches at night to make maps of the area and conduct other **reconnaissance**.

The Navy also formed Underwater Demolition Teams (UDTs). Wearing swimming fins and face masks, UDTs located underwater **obstacles** that could get in the way of American boats, such as coral reefs or enemy mines. These underwater teams were nicknamed "frogmen" for their ability to operate on land and in water.

UDTs fought in the Korean War (1950–1953). They swam to shore ahead of invading troops, scouting for mines and clearing obstacles. They also marched inland to blow up enemy bridges.

The First SEALs

The success of early units such as the Scouts and Raiders and UDTs led to the creation of the Navy SEALs. President John F. Kennedy decided the Navy should have a **permanent** special force that was ready to conduct special operations anywhere and at any time. In 1962, the Navy formed SEAL Teams One and Two. The first SEALs saw action right away, in the Vietnam War (1957–1975). SEALs were sent behind enemy lines to destroy supplies and capture enemy leaders.

Small teams of SEALs, such as this one, carried out many dangerous missions in Vietnam.

During the Vietnam War, American troops tried to stop **Communist** forces from taking over Vietnam. However, Communists eventually took control of the country in 1975.

The story of a SEAL fighter named Bob Kerrey shows just how dangerous some of the missions in Vietnam were. One morning before dawn in 1969, Bob and his team climbed a 350-foot (107 m) cliff. They hoped to surprise an enemy camp. The enemy **ambushed** the SEALs, however, and Bob was badly wounded by a **grenade**. Even as blood flowed from his leg, Bob continued to lead his men and completed the mission. He was later given the Medal of Honor, the country's highest military honor.

Bob Kerrey when he was training to become a SEAL

Bob Kerrey later served as a U.S. Senator from Nebraska from 1989 to 2001.

SEAL Team Six

In the years since the Vietnam War, Navy SEALs have **adapted** to face new challenges around the world. In 1979, students in the Middle Eastern country of Iran seized 52 Americans and held them as **hostages**. American forces attempted to rescue the hostages but failed. As a result, military leaders decided a new SEAL team was needed to fight terrorists. This **elite** new team would be known as SEAL Team Six.

American hostages held in Iran

At the time Team Six was created, there were only two other SEAL teams. The name "Team Six" was chosen to confuse America's enemies about how many SEAL teams actually exist.

What makes the members of Team Six different from other SEALs? For one thing, the names of Team Six members are top secret. These men are specially trained to carry out the most difficult secret missions, such as hunting down terrorists and rescuing hostages. It's believed that SEAL Team Six has about 300 members—but no records about this team are made public.

The Navy will not reveal the names of Team Six members. In photos, their faces are blurred to hide their identities.

So You Want to Be a SEAL?

How do SEALs prepare to carry out their dangerous missions? The answer is simple: years of training. In fact, the training required to become a SEAL is considered the toughest in the entire U.S. military.

Obstacle courses are a big part of SEAL training.

Before **candidates** even begin SEAL training, they must pass this fitness test—with just a few minutes to rest between each exercise:

✔ Swim 500 yards (457 m) in 12 minutes, 30 seconds or less

✔ Complete at least 42 push-ups in less than 2 minutes

✔ Complete at least 50 sit-ups in less than 2 minutes

✔ Complete at least 6 pull-ups

✔ Run 1.5 miles (2.4 km) in less than 11 minutes, 30 seconds

Because SEAL training is so difficult, most candidates drop out. Only about one third of those who begin the training make it to the end and become SEALs.

Any male member of the Navy who is 28 years old or younger can volunteer to become a SEAL. Once accepted into the program, the training begins with seven weeks of **brutal** workouts. The **dreaded** week four—called "hell week"—is the hardest. During this time, SEAL candidates run, swim, crawl through mud, and carry boats over their heads for twenty hours a day. The men must also survive on a total of just four hours of sleep over five and a half days of training.

In the so-called "surf torture" exercise, candidates lie in freezing ocean waters and then jump up and exercise in wet clothes.

Just Getting Started

Even **trainees** who make it through the seven weeks still face many more months of challenges. For example, they must complete seven weeks of swimming and scuba training, which includes the "drown-proofing" test. To pass this test, a candidate must be able to swim, dive, and float in the water—with his hands and feet tied together!

Navy SEALS training in the ocean

The next seven-week course focuses on land warfare. Trainees practice rock climbing, hand-to-hand combat, and **navigation** with a map, compass, and **GPS** equipment. They also learn how to use a variety of weapons and explosives. All the while, they must continue to pass timed fitness tests every week. Candidates then move on to three weeks of parachute training, where they jump from helicopters and planes that are at least as high as 9,500 feet (2,896 m) in the air.

SEALs use buildings like this one to train for fighting in cities.

Teamwork is one of the most important things that SEALs learn. No SEAL has ever been left behind on a mission.

19

Joining Team Six

Candidates who complete land warfare training then begin the fifteen-week SEAL Qualification Training (SQT). During this time, candidates improve on the skills they have learned. Those who successfully complete SQT officially become Navy SEALs and report to their assigned team—where they begin another year and a half of training! If SEALs perform successfully for several years, they can become candidates for Team Six.

These SEALs are practicing "fast-roping"—sliding down ropes from a helicopter.

All together, SEAL candidates must complete more than 30 months of training before they are ready to carry out missions.

Men are awarded this Trident pin when they become Navy SEALs.

Joining Team Six requires even more training. The SEALs must learn to master difficult parachute jumps and scuba dives. Using a building called a "shooting house," candidates practice charging into rooms and shooting targets. All of these skills are critical for members of Team Six. Since the terrorist attacks of September 11, 2001, the SEAL Team Six missions have focused on capturing terrorists and destroying their weapons.

The hunt for terrorists has taken SEAL Team Six deep into the mountains of Afghanistan, where many terrorist leaders hid after the September 11 attacks.

Attacked by Pirates

While SEALs have focused on fighting terrorism since 2001, they have carried out other kinds of missions as well. In April 2009, armed pirates from Somalia stormed aboard an American **cargo** ship, the *Maersk Alabama,* in the Indian Ocean. The pirates grabbed the ship's captain, Richard Phillips, and escaped on an 18-foot (5 m) boat. They demanded a huge **ransom**, saying, "If we don't get what we want, we will kill the captain."

The *Maersk Alabama* loaded with cargo

At the time of the pirate attack, the *Maersk Alabama* was headed for Kenya, full of food to aid the hungry. The pirates hoped to steal and sell the valuable cargo.

President Barack Obama ordered the military to rescue Captain Phillips. To carry out the mission, a Navy plane flew Team Six members high above the Indian Ocean. The SEALs pushed inflatable boats out of the plane. Then they jumped out themselves and parachuted down to the water. They swam to their boats, climbed into them, and were soon picked up by a Navy destroyer, the USS *Bainbridge*. Once aboard the Navy ship, the SEALs formed their plan.

Yemen

Somalia

Ethiopia

Kenya

Where pirates stormed aboard the *Maersk Alabama*

Indian Ocean

Arctic Ocean

NORTH AMERICA

EUROPE

ASIA

Atlantic Ocean

AFRICA

Pacific Ocean

Pacific Ocean

SOUTH AMERICA

Indian Ocean

AUSTRALIA

N
W E
S

Southern Ocean

ANTARCTICA

Three Perfect Shots

From the deck of the *Bainbridge,* the SEALs could see the small boat on which the pirates held Captain Phillips. There were three pirates, each holding a gun. The captain was tied up. The three SEALs loaded their **sniper rifles** and aimed at the pirates. They knew they would each have only one shot. If any of them missed, the surviving pirate would surely kill Captain Phillips.

From the back of this Navy destroyer, the *Bainbridge,* SEAL snipers fired at the three pirates on the small red boat.

Each SEAL picked a target. When the pirate boat was within about 100 feet (30 m), the three SEALs fired at the exact same time. All three bullets hit their targets—and the pirates were killed. Crew members of the *Bainbridge* then rescued Captain Phillips and brought him to safety aboard the American ship.

Captain Phillips (right) after his rescue, with the commander of the *Bainbridge*

In recent years, SEALs have completed missions in countries around the world, including Panama, Kuwait, Somalia, and Bosnia.

The Front Lines of Freedom

Just two years after the rescue of Captain Phillips, SEAL Team Six took down the terrorist leader Osama bin Laden. Since then, the tough assignments have continued. In January 2012, Team Six members were given another rescue mission. Pirates in Somalia had seized an American woman and a Danish man, and were demanding millions of dollars in ransom. To save the hostages, SEALs used parachutes to drop down in the middle of the night, charge into the pirate hideout, and rescue the victims.

SEALs learn to parachute during their training so that they can use the skill in rescue missions.

Because Team Six operations are top secret, the American public will never know about most of their missions. Americans do know, however, that Team Six continues to take on dangerous jobs around the world. "We may not always know their names," said President Barack Obama, thanking SEAL Team Six. "We may not always know their stories, but they are there every day on the front lines of freedom."

Navy SEALs expect every day to be a challenge. SEALs have a saying: "The only easy day was yesterday."

The official name for SEAL Team Six is the Naval Special Warfare Development Group, or DEVGRU for short.

SEAL Team Six's Gear

To carry out missions at sea, in the air, and on land,
SEAL Team Six relies on a wide variety of equipment.
Here are some of the weapons and gear they use.

Scuba gear allows SEALs to conduct missions underwater or to swim up to a target without being detected.

Combat rubber raiding craft are small inflatable boats that can be dropped by parachutes from planes or carried over land by SEALs.

The **M4A1 carbine** is fitted with a grenade launcher.

The **M-14** is a battle rifle.

The **M136 AT4** shoots anti-tank rockets.

Glossary

adapted (uh-DAP-tid) changed in order to face new settings and challenges

Al Qaeda (AHL KAY-duh) the terrorist group that was responsible for the September 11 attacks on the United States

ambushed (AM-busht) attacked from a hidden position

brutal (BROO-tuhl) extremely tough or difficult

candidates (KAN-duh-dayts) people who are hoping to get a certain job

cargo (KAR-goh) items that are delivered by plane, truck, or ship

Communist (KOM-yuh-nist) having to do with a type of government where the government owns all goods and property

compound (KOM-pound) a fenced-in area with buildings inside

dreaded (DRED-id) feared

elite (i-LEET) chosen as the best

enemy lines (EN-uh-mee LYENZ) areas of land from where the enemy fights

GPS (jee-pee-ESS) letters standing for Global Positioning System; a space-based navigation satellite system that provides accurate location information

grenade (gruh-NAYD) a small bomb that is usually thrown by hand

hostages (HOSS-tij-iz) people who are held as prisoners as a way of demanding money or other things

intelligence (in-TEL-uh-juhnss) information about an enemy

military leaders (MIL-uh-*ter*-ee LEE-durs) the people who are in charge of a country's soldiers and armed forces

navigation (nav-uh-GAY-shuhn) to find one's way from place to place

obstacles (OB-stuh-kuhlz) things that block a path

parachute (PA-ruh-*shoot*) to jump out of a plane or helicopter using a soft cloth attached to nylon lines to slow down the fall

permanent (PUR-muh-nuhnt) created to last forever

ransom (RAN-suhm) money demanded in return for setting a kidnapped or captive person free

reconnaissance (rih-KON-uh-suhns) the gathering of information about an enemy

scuba dive (SKOO-buh DIVE) deep underwater diving using special breathing equipment

sniper rifles (SNYE-pur RYE-fuhls) guns used by a skilled shooter who is trained to shoot enemy fighters from a hidden position

special operations forces (SPESH-uhl *op*-uh-RAY-shuhnz FORSS-iz) groups of highly skilled soldiers in the military; called *special ops* for short

terrain (tuh-RAYN) a type of land surface

terrorist (TER-ur-ist) a group that uses violence and threats to achieve its goals

trainees (tray-NEEZ) people who are learning to do something by practicing

Bibliography

Axe, David. "8,000 Miles, 96 Hours, 3 Dead Pirates: Inside a Navy SEAL Rescue." *Wired* (October 17, 2012).

Owen, Mark, with Kevin Maurer. *No Easy Day: The Autobiography of a Navy SEAL.* New York: Dutton (2012).

U.S. Navy Web Site: Naval Special Warfare Command (http://www.public.navy.mil/nsw/Pages/History.aspx)

Wasdin, Howard E., and Stephen Templin. *SEAL Team Six: Memoirs of an Elite Navy SEAL Sniper.* New York: St. Martin's Press (2011).

Read More

David, Jack. *Navy SEALs (Torque: Armed Forces).* Minneapolis, MN: Bellwether Media (2009).

Lunis, Natalie. *The Takedown of Osama bin Laden (Special Ops).* New York: Bearport (2012).

Nelson, Drew. *Navy SEALs (US Special Forces).* New York: Gareth Stevens (2012).

Yomtov, Nel. *Navy SEALs in Action (Special Ops).* New York: Bearport (2008).

Learn More Online

To learn more about Navy SEAL Team Six, visit
www.bearportpublishing.com/SpecialOpsII

Index

About the Author

Stephen Person has written many children's books about history, science, and the environment.